A Study of the T Relation to the Development of Form and Ornament

Sixth Annual Report of the Bureau of Ethnology to the Secretary of the Smithsonian Institution, 1884-'85, Government Printing Office, Washington, 1888, (pages 189-252)

William Henry Holmes

Alpha Editions

This edition published in 2024

ISBN : 9789364730228

Design and Setting By
Alpha Editions
www.alphaedis.com
Email - info@alphaedis.com

As per information held with us this book is in Public Domain.
This book is a reproduction of an important historical work. Alpha Editions uses the
best technology to reproduce historical work in the same manner it was first
published to preserve its original nature. Any marks or number seen are left
intentionally to preserve its true form.

INTRODUCTION.

The textile art is one of the most ancient known, dating back to the very inception of culture. In primitive times it occupied a wide field, embracing the stems of numerous branches of industry now expressed in other materials or relegated to distinct systems of construction. Accompanying the gradual narrowing of its sphere there was a steady development with the general increase of intelligence and skill so that with the cultured nations of to-day it takes an important, though unobtrusive, place in the hierarchy of the arts.

Woven fabrics include all those products of art in which the elements or parts employed in construction are largely filamental and are combined by methods conditioned chiefly by their flexibility. The processes employed are known by such terms as interlacing, plaiting, netting, weaving, sewing, and embroidering.

The materials used at first are chiefly filiform vegetal growths, such as twigs, leaves, roots, and grasses, but later on filiform and then fibrous elements from all the kingdoms of nature, as well as numerous artificial preparations, are freely used. These are employed in the single, doubled, doubled and twisted, and plaited conditions, and are combined by the hands alone, by the hands assisted by simple devices, by hand looms, and finally in civilization by machine looms.

The products are, first, individual structures or articles, such as shelters, baskets, nets, and garments, or integral parts of these; and, second, "piece" goods, such as are not adapted to use until they are cut and fitted. In earlier stages of art we have to deal almost exclusively with the former class, as the tailor and the house furnisher are evolved with civilization.

In their bearing upon art these products are to be studied chiefly with reference to three grand divisions of phenomena, the first of which I shall denominate *constructive*, the second *functional*, and the third *esthetic*. The last class, with which this paper has almost exclusively to deal, is composed mainly of what may be called the superconstructive and superfunctional features of the art and includes three subdivisions of phenomena, connected respectively with (1) form, (2) color, and (3) design. Esthetic features of form are, in origin and manifestation, related to both function and construction; color and design, to construction mainly. In the following study separate sections are given to each of these topics.

It is fortunate perhaps that in this work I am restricted to the products of rather primitive stages of culture, as I have thus to deal with a limited number of uses, simple processes, and simple shapes. In the advanced stages of art we encounter complex phenomena, processes, and conditions, the accumulation of ages, through which no broad light can fall upon the field of vision.

In America there is a vast body of primitive, indigenous art having no parallel in the world. Uncontaminated by contact with the complex conditions of civilized art, it offers the best possible facilities for the study of the fundamental principles of esthetic development.

The laws of evolution correspond closely in all art, and, if once rightly interpreted in the incipient stage of a single, homogeneous culture, are traceable with comparative ease through all the succeeding stages of civilization.

FORM IN TEXTILE ART.

Form in the textile art, as in all other useful arts, is fundamentally, although not exclusively, the resultant or expression of function, but at the same time it is further than in other shaping arts from expressing the whole of function. Such is the pliability of a large portion of textile products—as, for example, nets, garments, and hangings—that the shapes assumed are variable, and, therefore, when not distended or for some purpose folded or draped, the articles are without esthetic value or interest. The more rigid objects, in common with the individuals of other useful arts, while their shape still accords with their functional office, exhibit attributes of form generally recognized as pleasing to the mind, which are expressed by the terms grace, elegance, symmetry, and the like. Such attributes are not separable from functional attributes, but originate and exist conjointly with them.

In addition to these features of form we observe others of a more decidedly superfunctional character, added manifestly for the purpose of enhancing the appearance.

In very primitive times when a utensil is produced functional ideas predominate, and there is, perhaps, so far as its artificial characters are concerned, a minimum of comeliness. But as the ages pass by essential features are refined and elements of beauty are added and emphasized. In riper culture the growing pressure of esthetic desire leads to the addition of many superficial modifications whose chief office is to please the fancy. In periods of deadened sensibility or even through the incompetence of individual artists in any period, such features may be ill chosen and erroneously applied, interfering with construction and use, and thus violating well founded and generally accepted canons of taste. In respect to primitive works we may distinguish four steps in the acquisition of esthetic features of form, three of which are normal, the fourth abnormal: First, we have that in which functional characters alone are considered, any element of beauty, whether due to the artist's hand or to the accidents of material, construction, or model, being purely adventitious; second, that in which the necessary features of the utensil appear to have experienced the supervision of taste, edges being rounded, curves refined, and symmetry perfected; third, that in which the functionally perfect object, just described, undergoes further variations of contour, adding to variety, unity, &c., thus enhancing beauty without interfering with serviceability; and, fourth, that in which, under abnormal influences, beauty is sought at the sacrifice of functional and constructive perfection.

FIG. 286. Mat or tray exhibiting a minimum of esthetic attributes of form. Moki work—1/8.

The exact relations of the various classes of forces and phenomena pertaining to this theme may be more fully elucidated by the aid of illustrations. Woven mats, in early use by many tribes of men and originating in the attempt to combine leaves, vines, and branches for purposes of comfort, are flat because of function, the degree of flatness depending upon the size of filaments and mode of combination; and in outline they are irregular, square, round, or oval, as a result of many causes and influences, embracing use, construction, material, models, &c. A close approach to symmetry, where not imposed by some of the above mentioned agencies, is probably due to esthetic tendencies on the part of the artist. The esthetic interest attaching to such a shape cannot be great, unless perhaps it be regarded, as all individuals and classes may be regarded, in its possible relations to preceding, associated, and succeeding forms of art. The varied features observed upon the surface, the colors and patterns (Fig. 286), pertain to design rather than to form and will receive attention in the proper place.

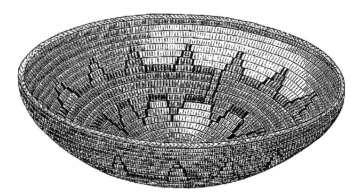

FIG. 287. Tray having decided esthetic attributes of form. Obtained from the Apache—1/2.

In point of contour the basket tray shown in Fig. 287 has a somewhat more decided claim upon esthetic attention than the preceding, as the curves exhibited mark a step of progress in complexity and grace. How much of this is due to intention and how much to technical perfection must remain in doubt. In work so perfect we are wont, however unwarrantably, to recognize the influence of taste.

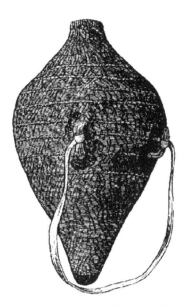

FIG. 288. Pyriform water vessel used by the Piute Indians—1/8.

A third example—presented in Fig. 288—illustrates an advanced stage in the art of basketry and exhibits a highly specialized shape. The forces and influences concerned in its evolution may be analyzed as follows: A primal origin in function and a final adaptation to a special function, the carrying and storing of water; a contour full to give capacity, narrow above for safety, and pointed below that it may be set in sand; curves kept within certain bounds by the limitations of construction; and a goodly share of variety, symmetry, and grace, the result to a certain undetermined extent of the esthetic tendencies of the artist's mind. In regard to the last point there is generally in forms so simple an element of uncertainty; but many examples may be found in which there is positive evidence of the existence of a strong desire on the part of the primitive basketmaker to enhance beauty of form. It will be observed that the textile materials and construction do not lend themselves freely to minuteness in detail or to complexity of outline, especially in those small ways in which beauty is most readily expressed.

Modifications of a decidedly esthetic character are generally suggested to the primitive mind by some functional, constructive, or accidental feature which may with ease be turned in the new direction. In the vessel presented in Fig. 289—the work of Alaskan Indians—the margin is varied by altering the relations of the three marginal turns of the coil, producing a scalloped effect. This is without reference to use, is uncalled for in construction, and hence is, in all probability, the direct result of esthetic tendencies. Other and much more elaborate examples may be found in the basketry of almost all countries.

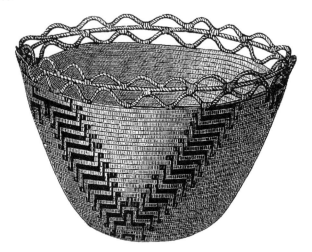

FIG. 289. Vessel with esthetic characters of form. Work of the Yakama—1/4.

In the pursuit of this class of enrichment there is occasionally noticeable a tendency to overload the subject with extraneous details. This is not apt to occur, however, in the indigenous practice of an art, but comes more frequently from a loss of equilibrium or balance in motives or desires, caused by untoward exotic influence. When, through suggestions derived from contact with civilized art, the savage undertakes to secure all the grace and complexity observed in the works of more cultured peoples, he does so at the expense of construction and adaptability to use. An example of such work is presented in Fig. 290, a weak, useless, and wholly vicious piece of basketry. Other equally meretricious pieces represent goblets, bottles, and tea pots. They are the work of the Indians of the northwest coast and are executed in the neatest possible manner, bearing evidence of the existence of cultivated taste.

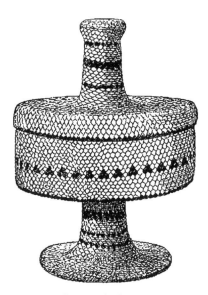

FIG. 290. Basket made under foreign influence, construction and use being sacrificed to fancied beauty—1/3.

It appears from the preceding analyses that *form* in this art is not sufficiently sensitive to receive impressions readily from the delicate touch of esthetic fingers; besides, there are peculiar difficulties in the way of detecting traces of the presence and supervision of taste. The inherent morphologic forces of the art are strong and stubborn and tend to produce the precise classes of results that we, at this stage of culture, are inclined to attribute to esthetic influence. If, in the making of a vessel, the demands of use are fully satisfied, if construction is perfect of its kind, if materials are uniformly suitable, and if models are not absolutely bad, it follows that the result must necessarily possess in a high degree those very attributes that all agree are pleasing to the eye.

In a primitive water vessel function gives a full outline, as capacity is a prime consideration; convenience of use calls for a narrow neck and a conical base; construction and materials unite to impose certain limitations to curves and their combinations, from which the artist cannot readily free himself. Models furnished by nature, as they are usually graceful, do not interfere with the preceding agencies, and all these forces united tend to give symmetry, grace, and the unity that belongs to simplicity. Taste which is in a formative state can but fall in with these tendencies of the art, and must be led by them, and led in a measure corresponding to their persistency and universality. If the textile art had been the only one known to man, ideas of the esthetic in shape would have been in a great measure formed through that art. Natural forms would have had little to do with it except through models furnished directly to and utilized by the art, for the ideas of primitive men concentrate about that upon which their hands work and upon which their thoughts from necessity dwell with steady attention from generation to generation.

RELATIONS OF FORM TO ORNAMENT.

It would seem that the esthetic tendencies of the mind, failing to find satisfactory expression in shape, seized upon the non-essential features of the art—markings of the surface and color of filaments—creating a new field in which to labor and expending their energy upon ornament.

Shape has some direct relations to ornament, and these relations may be classified as follows:

First, the contour of the vessel controls its ornament to a large extent, dictating the positions of design and setting its limits; figures are in stripes, zones, rays, circles, ovals, or rectangles—according, in no slight measure, to the character of the spaces afforded by details of contour. Secondly, it affects ornament through the reproduction and repetition of features of form, such as handles, for ornamental purposes. Thirdly, it is probable that shape influences embellishment through the peculiar bias given by it to the taste and judgment of men prior to or independent of the employment of ornament.

COLOR IN TEXTILE ART.

Color is one of the most constant factors in man's environment, and it is so strongly and persistently forced upon his attention, so useful as a means of identification and distinction, that it necessarily receives a large share of consideration. It is probably one of the foremost objective agencies in the formation and development of the esthetic sense.

The natural colors of textile materials are enormously varied and form one of the chief attractions of the products of the art. The great interest taken in color—the great importance attached to it—is attested by the very general use of dyes, by means of which additional variety and brilliancy of effect are secured.

Color employed in the art is not related to use, excepting, perhaps, in symbolic and superstitious matters; nor is it of consequence in construction, although it derives importance from the manner in which construction causes it to be manifested to the eye. It finds its chief use in the field of design, in making evident to the eye the figures with which objects of art are embellished.

Color is employed or applied in two distinct ways: it is woven or worked into the fabric by using colored filaments or parts, or it is added to the surface of the completed object by means of pencils, brushes, and dies. Its employment in the latter manner is especially convenient when complex ideographic or pictorial subjects are to be executed.

TEXTILE ORNAMENT.

DEVELOPMENT OF A GEOMETRIC SYSTEM OF DESIGN WITHIN THE ART.

INTRODUCTION.

Having made a brief study of form and color in the textile art, I shall now present the great group or family of phenomena whose exclusive office is that of enhancing beauty. It will be necessary, however, to present, besides those features of the art properly expressive of the esthetic culture of the race, all those phenomena that, being present in the art without man's volition, tend to suggest decorative conceptions and give shape to them. I shall show how the latter class of features arise as a necessity of the art, how they gradually come into notice and are seized upon by the esthetic faculty, and how under its guidance they assist in the development of a system of ornament of world wide application.

For convenience of treatment esthetic phenomena may be classed as *relieved* and *flat*. Figures or patterns of a relievo nature arise during construction as a result of the intersections and other more complex relations—the bindings—of the warp and woof or of inserted or applied elements. Flat or surface features are manifested in color, either in unison with or independent of the relieved details. Such is the nature of the textile art that in its ordinary practice certain combinations of both classes of features go on as a necessity of the art and wholly without reference to the desire of the artist or to the effect of resultant patterns upon the eye. The character of such figures depends upon the kind of construction and upon the accidental association of natural colors in construction.

At some period of the practice of the art these peculiar, adventitious surface characters began to attract attention and to be cherished for the pleasure they gave; what were at first adventitious features now took on functions peculiar to themselves, for they were found to gratify desires distinct from those cravings that arise directly from physical wants.

It is not to be supposed for a moment that the inception of esthetic notions dates from this association of ideas of beauty with textile characters. Long before textile objects of a high class were made, ideas of an esthetic nature had been entertained by the mind, as, for example, in connection with personal adornment. The skin had been painted, pendants placed about the neck, and bright feathers set in the hair to enhance attractiveness, and it is not difficult to conceive of the transfer of such ideas from purely personal associations to the embellishment of articles intimately associated with the person. No matter, however, what the period or manner of the association of such ideas with the textile art, that association may be taken as the datum point in the development of a great system of decoration whose distinguishing characters are the result of the geometric textile construction.

In amplifying this subject I find it convenient to treat separately the two classes of decorative phenomena—the relieved and the flat— notwithstanding the fact that they are for the most part intimately associated and act together in the accomplishment of a common end.

RELIEF PHENOMENA.

Ordinary features.—The relieved surface characters of fabrics resulting from construction and available for decoration are more or less distinctly perceptible to the eye and to the touch and are susceptible of unlimited variation in detail and arrangement. Such features are familiar to all in the strongly marked ridges of basketry, and much more pleasingly so in the delicate figures of damasks, embroideries, and laces. So long as the figures produced are confined exclusively to the necessary features of unembellished construction, as is the case in very primitive work and in all plain work, the resultant patterns are wholly geometric and by endless repetition of like parts extremely monotonous.

In right angled weaving the figures combine in straight lines, which run parallel or cross at uniform distances and angles. In radiate weaving, as in basketry, the radial lines are crossed in an equally formal manner by concentric lines. In other classes of combination there is an almost equal degree of geometricity.

When, however, with the growth of intelligence and skill it is found that greater variety of effect can be secured by modifying the essential combinations of parts, and that, too, without interfering with constructive perfection or with use, a new and wide field is opened for the developmental tendencies of textile decoration.

Moreover, in addition to the facilities afforded by the necessary elements of construction, there are many extraneous resources of which the textile decorator may freely avail himself. The character of these is such that the results, however varied, harmonize thoroughly with indigenous textile forms.

To make these points quite clear it will be necessary to analyze somewhat closely the character and scope of textile combination and of the resultant and associated phenomena.

We may distinguish two broad classes of constructive phenomena made use of in the expression of relieved enrichment. As indicated above, these are, first, essential or actual constructive features and, second, extra or superconstructive features.

First, it is found that in the practice of primitive textile art a variety of methods of combination or bindings of the parts have been evolved and utilized, and we observe that each of these—no matter what the material or what the size and character of the filamental elements—gives rise to distinct classes of surface effects. Thus it appears that peoples who happen to discover and use like combinations produce kindred decorative results, while those employing unlike constructions achieve distinct classes of surface embellishment. These constructive peculiarities have a pretty decided effect upon the style of ornament, relieved or colored, and must be carefully considered in the treatment of design; but it is found that each type of combination has a greatly varied capacity of expression, tending to obliterate sharp lines of demarkation between the groups of results. It sometimes even happens that in distinct types of weaving almost identical surface effects are produced.

It will not be necessary in this connection to present a full series of the fundamental bindings or orders of combination, as a few will suffice to illustrate the principles involved and to make clear the bearing of this class of phenomena upon decoration. I choose, first, a number of examples from the simplest type of weaving, that in which the web and the woof are merely interlaced, the filaments crossing at right angles or nearly so. In Fig. 291 we have the result exhibited in a plain open or reticulated fabric constructed from ordinary untwisted fillets, such as are employed in our splint and cane products. Fig. 292 illustrates the surface produced by crowding the horizontal series of the same fabric close together, so that the vertical series is entirely hidden. The surface here exhibits a succession of vertical ribs, an effect totally distinct from that seen in the preceding example. The third variety (Fig. 293) differs but slightly from the first. The fillets are wider and are set close together without crowding, giving the surface a checkered appearance.

FIG. 291. Surface relief in simplest form of intersection.

FIG. 293. Surface relief produced by wide fillets set close together.

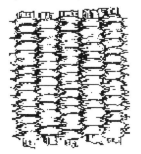

FIG. 292. Surface relief produced by horizontal series crowded together.

The second variety of surface effect is that most frequently seen in the basketry of our western tribes, as it results from the great degree of compactness necessary in vessels intended to contain liquids, semiliquid foods, or pulverized substances. The general surface effect given by closely woven work is illustrated in Fig. 294, which represents a large wicker carrying basket obtained from the Moki Indians. In this instance the ridges, due to a heavy series of radiating warp filaments, are seen in a vertical position.

FIG. 294. Basket showing ribbed surface produced by impacting the horizontal or concentric filaments. Moki work—1/8.

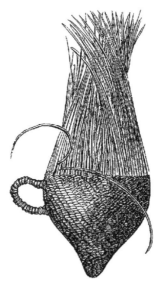

FIG. 295. Alternation of intersection, producing oblique or spiral ribs. Piute work—1/8.

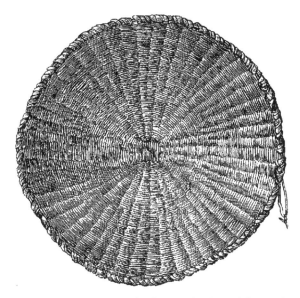

FIG. 296. Radiating ribs as seen in flat work viewed from above. Moki work—1/4.

It will be observed, however, that the ridges do not necessarily take the direction of the warp filaments, for, with a different alternation of the horizontal series—the woof—we get oblique ridges, as shown in the partly finished bottle illustrated in Fig. 295. They are, however, not so pronounced as in the preceding case. The peculiar effect of radiate and concentric weaving upon the ribs is well shown in Fig. 296.

By changes in the order of intersection, without changing the type of combination, we reach a series of results quite unlike the preceding; so distinct, indeed, that, abstracted from constructive relationships, there would be little suggestion of correlation. In the example given in Fig. 297 the series of filaments interlace, not by passing over and under alternate strands, as in the preceding set of examples, but by extending over and under a number of the opposing series at each step and in such order as to give wide horizontal ridges ribbed diagonally.

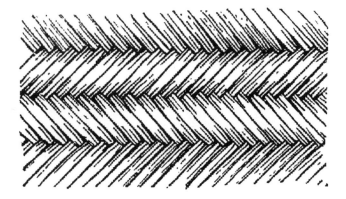

FIG. 297. Diagonal combination, giving herring bone effect.

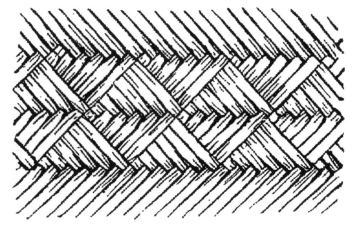

FIG. 298. Elaboration of diagonal combination, giving triangular figures.

This example is from an ancient work basket obtained at Ancon, Peru, and shown in Fig. 299. The surface features are in strong relief, giving a pronounced herring bone effect.

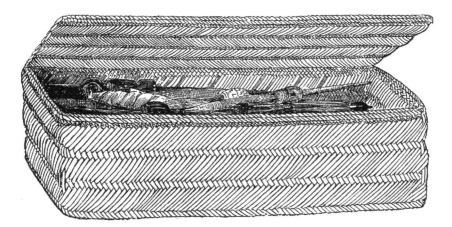

FIG. 299. Peruvian work basket of reeds, with strongly relieved ridges.

Slight changes in the succession of parts enable the workman to produce a great variety of decorative patterns, an example of which is shown in Fig. 298. A good illustration is also seen in Fig. 286, and another piece, said to be of Seminole workmanship, is given in Fig. 300. These and similar relieved results are fruitful sources of primitive decorative motives. They are employed not only within the art itself, but in many other arts less liberally supplied with suggestions of embellishment.

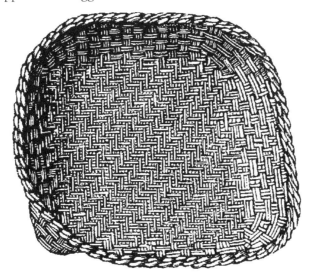

FIG. 300. Effects produced by varying the order of intersection. Seminole work—1/8.

Taking a second type of combination, we have a family of resultant patterns in the main distinguishable from the preceding.

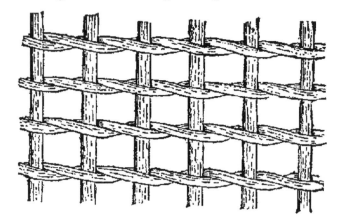

FIG. 301. Surface effect in open twined combination.

FIG. 302. Surface effect of twined, lattice combination in basketry of the Clallam Indians of Washington Territory—1/8.

Fig. 301 illustrates the simplest form of what Dr. O.T. Mason has called the twined combination, a favorite one with many of our native tribes. The strands of the woof series are arranged in twos and in weaving are twisted half around at each intersection, inclosing the opposing fillets. The resulting open work has much the appearance of ordinary netting, and when of pliable materials and distended or strained over an earthen or gourd vessel the pattern exhibited is strikingly suggestive of decoration. The result of this combination upon a lattice foundation of rigid materials is well shown in the large basket presented in Fig. 302. Other variants of this type are given in the three succeeding figures.

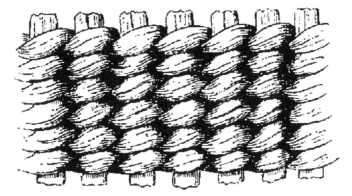

FIG. 303. Surface effect in impacted work of twined combination.

The result seen in Fig. 303 is obtained by impacting the horizontal or twined series of threads. The surface is nearly identical with that of the closely impacted example of the preceding type (Fig. 292). The peculiarities are more marked when colors are used. When the doubled and twisted series of strands are placed far apart and the opposing series are laid side by side a pleasing result is given, as shown in Fig. 304 and in the body of the conical basket illustrated in Fig. 307.

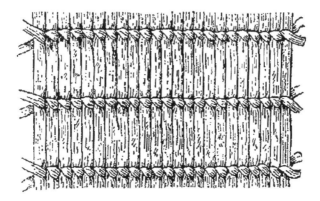

FIG. 304. Surface effect obtained by placing the warp strands close together and the woof cables far apart.

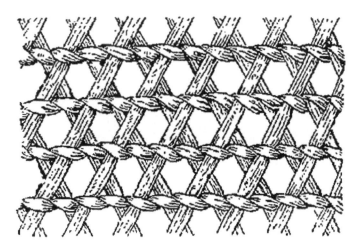

FIG. 305. Surface effect obtained by crossing the warp series in open twined work.

In Fig. 305 we have a peculiar diagonally crossed arrangement of the untwisted series of filaments, giving a lattice work effect.

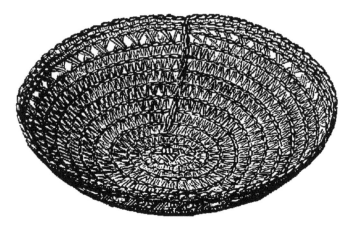

FIG. 306. Decorative effects produced by variations in the radiate or warp series in an open work tray. Klamath work—1/4.

Fig. 306 serves to show how readily this style of weaving lends itself to the production of decorative modification, especially in the direction of the concentric zonal arrangement so universal in vessel-making arts.

The examples given serve to indicate the unlimited decorative resources possessed by the art without employing any but legitimate constructive elements, and it will be seen that still wider results can be obtained by combining two or more varieties or styles of binding in the construction and the embellishment of a single object or in the same piece of fabric. A good, though very simple, illustration of this is shown in the tray or mat presented in Fig. 286. In this case a border, varying from the center portion in appearance, is obtained by changing one series of the filaments from a multiple to a single arrangement.

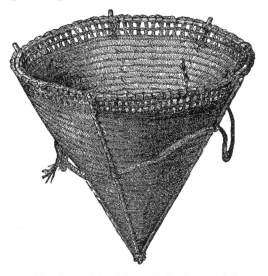

FIG. 307. Conical basket of the Klamath Indians of Oregon, showing peculiar twined effect and an open work border—1/8.

The conical basket shown in Fig. 307 serves to illustrate the same point. In this case a rudely worked, though effective, border is secured by changing the angle of the upright series near the top and combining them by plaiting, and in such a way as to leave a border of open work.

Now the two types of construction, the interlaced and the twined, some primitive phases of which have been reviewed and illustrated, as they are carried forward in the technical progress of the art, exhibit many new features of combination and resultant surface character, but the elaboration is in all cases along lines peculiar to these types of weaving.

Other types of combination of web and woof, all tapestry, and all braiding, netting, knitting, crochet, and needle work exhibit characters peculiar to themselves, developing distinct groups of relieved results; yet all are analogous in principle to those already illustrated and unite in carrying forward the same great geometric system of combination.

Reticulated work.—A few paragraphs may be added here in regard to reticulated fabrics of all classes of combination, as they exhibit more than usually interesting relievo phenomena and have a decided bearing upon the growth of ornament.

In all the primitive weaving with which we are acquainted definite reticulated patterns are produced by variations in the spacings and other relations of the warp and woof; and the same is true in all the higher forms of the art. The production of reticulated work is the especial function of netting, knitting, crocheting, and certain varieties of needlework, and a great diversity of relieved results are produced, no figure being too complex and no form too pronounced to be undertaken by ambitious workmen.

In the following figures we have illustrations of the peculiar class of primitive experiments that, after the lapse of ages, lead up to marvelous results, the highest of which may be found in the exquisite laces of cultured peoples. The Americans had only taken the first steps in this peculiar art, but the results are on this account of especial interest in the history of the art.

An example of simple reticulated hand weaving is shown in Fig. 308. It is the work of the mound builders and is taken from an impression upon an ancient piece of pottery obtained in Tennessee.

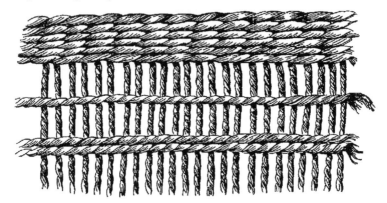

FIG. 308. Incipient stage of reticulated ornament. Fabric of the mound builders.

Fig. 309 illustrates a bit of ancient Peruvian work executed on a frame or in a rude loom, a checker pattern being produced by arranging the warp and woof now close together and now wide apart.

Open work of this class is sometimes completed by after processes, certain threads or filaments being drawn out or introduced, by which means the figures are emphasized and varied.

In Fig. 310 we have a second Peruvian example in which the woof threads have been omitted for the space of an inch, and across this interval the loose warp has been plaited and drawn together, producing a lattice-like band.

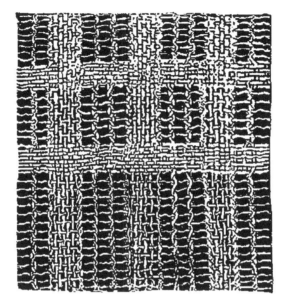

FIG. 309. Simple form of ornamental reticulation. Ancient Peruvian work.

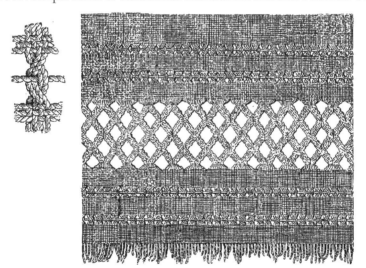

FIG. 310. Reticulated pattern in cotton cloth. Work of the ancient Peruvians.

In a similar way four other bands of narrow open work are introduced, two above and two below the wide band. These are produced by leaving the warp threads free for a short space and drawing alternate pairs across each other and fixing them so by means of a woof thread, as shown in the cut.

Examples of netting in which decorative features have been worked are found among the textile products of many American tribes and occur as well in several groups of ancient fabrics, but in most cases where designs of importance or complexity are desired parts are introduced to facilitate the work.

Superconstructive features.—These features, so important in the decoration of fabrics, are the result of devices by which a construction already capable of fulfilling the duties imposed by function has added to it parts intended to enhance beauty and which may or may not be of advantage to the fabric. They constitute one of the most widely used and effective resources of the textile decorator, and are added by sewing or stitching, inserting, drawing, cutting, applying, appending, &c. They add enormously to the capacity for producing relievo effects and make it possible even to render natural forms in the round. Notwithstanding this fact—the most important section of this class of features—embroidery is treated to better advantage under color phenomena, as color is very generally associated with the designs.

FIG. 311. Open work design embroidered upon a net-like fabric. From a grave at Ancon, Peru.

One example of lace-like embroidery may be given in this place. It is probably among the best examples of monochrome embroidery America has produced. In design and in method of realization it is identical with the rich, colored embroideries of the ancient Peruvians, being worked upon a net foundation, as shown in Fig. 311. The broad band of figures employs bird forms in connection with running geometric designs, and still more highly conventional bird forms are seen in the narrow band.

Appended ornaments are not amenable to the geometric laws of fabrication to the extent observed in other classes of ornament. They are, however, attached in ways consistent with the textile system, and are counted and spaced with great care, producing designs of a more or less pronounced geometric character. The work is a kind of embroidery, the parts employed being of the nature of pendants.

These include numberless articles derived from nature and art. It will suffice to present a few examples already at hand.

FIG. 312. Basket with pendent buckskin strands tipped with bits of tin. Apache Indians—1/8.

Fig. 312 illustrates a large, well made basket, the work of the Apache Indians. It serves to indicate the method of employing tassels and clustered pendants, which in this case consist of buckskin strings tipped with conical bits of tin. The checker pattern is in color.

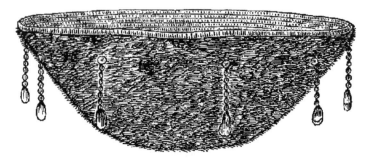

FIG. 313. Basket with pendants of beads and bits of shell, work of the northwest coast Indians.—1/4.

Fig. 313 illustrates the use of other varieties of pendants. A feather decked basket made by the northwest coast Indians is embellished with pendent ornaments consisting of strings of beads tipped with bits of bright shell. The importance of this class of work in higher forms of textiles may be illustrated by an example from Peru. It is probable that American art has produced few examples of tasseled work more wonderful than that of which a fragment is shown in Fig. 314. It is a fringed mantle, three feet in length and nearly the same in depth, obtained from an ancient tomb. The body is made up of separately woven bands, upon which disk-like and semilunar figures representing human faces are stitched, covering the surface in horizontal rows. To the center of these rosette-like parts clusters of tassels of varying sizes are attached. The fringe, which is twenty inches deep, is composed entirely of long strings of tassels, the larger tassels supporting clusters of smaller ones. There are upwards of three thousand tassels, the round heads of which are in many cases woven in colors, ridges, and nodes to represent the human features. The general color of the garment, which is of fine, silky wool, is a rich crimson. The illustration can convey only a hint of the complexity and beauty of the original.

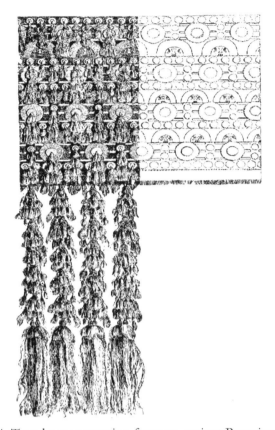

FIG. 314. Tassel ornamentation from an ancient Peruvian mantle.

We have now seen how varied and how striking are the surface characters of fabrics as expressed by the third dimension, by variation from a flat, featureless surface, and how all, essential and ornamental, are governed by the laws of geometric combination. We shall now see how these are related to color phenomena.

COLOR PHENOMENA.

Ordinary features.—In describing the constructive characters of fabrics and the attendant surface phenomena, I called attention to the fact that a greater part of the design manifested is enforced and supplemented by color, which gives new meaning to every feature. Color elements are present in the art from its very inception, and many simple patterns appear as accidents of textile aggregation long before the weaver or the possessor recognizes them as pleasing to the eye. When, finally, they are so recognized and a desire for greater elaboration springs up, the textile construction lends itself readily to the new office and under the esthetic forces brings about wonderful results without interfering in the least with the technical perfection of the articles embellished. But color is not confined to the mere emphasizing of figures already expressed in relief. It is capable of advancing alone into new fields, producing patterns and designs complex in arrangement and varied in hue, and that, too, without altering the simple, monotonous succession of relievo characters.

In color, as in relieved design, each species of constructive combination gives rise to more or less distinct groups of decorative results, which often become the distinguishing characteristics of the work of different peoples and the progenitors of long lines of distinctions in national decorative conceptions.

In addition to this apparently limitless capacity for expression, lovers of textile illumination have the whole series of extraordinary resources furnished by expedients not essential to ordinary construction, the character and scope of which have been dwelt upon to some extent in the preceding section.

I have already spoken of color in a general way, as to its necessary presence in art, its artificial application to fabrics and fabric materials, its symbolic characters, and its importance to esthetic progress. My object in this section is to indicate the part it takes in textile design, its methods of expression, the processes by which it advances in elaboration, and the part it takes in all geometric decoration.

It will be necessary, in the first place, to examine briefly the normal tendencies of color combination while still under the direct domination of constructive elaboration. In the way of illustration, let us take first a series of filaments, say in the natural color of the material, and pass through them in the simplest interlaced style a second series having a distinct color. A very simple geometric pattern is produced, as shown in Fig. 315. It is a sort of checker, an emphasized presentation of the relievo pattern shown in Fig. 291, the figures running horizontally, vertically, and diagonally. Had these filaments been accidentally associated in construction, the results might have been the same, but it is unnecessary to indicate in detail the possibilities of adventitious color combinations. So far as they exhibit system at all it is identical with the relievo elaboration.

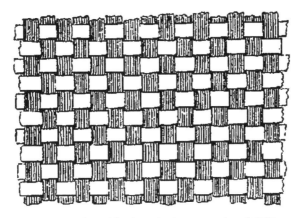

FIG. 315. Pattern produced by interlacing strands of different colors.

FIG. 316. Pattern produced by modifying the alternation of fillets.

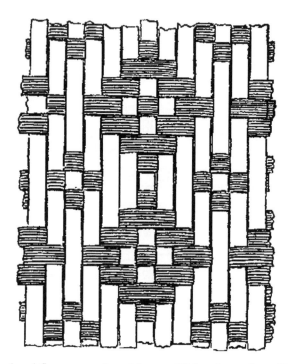

FIG. 317. Isolated figures produced by modifying the order of intersection.

Assuming that the idea of developing these figures into something more elaborate and striking is already conceived, let us study the processes and tendencies of growth. A very slight degree of ingenuity will enable the workman to vary the relation of the parts, producing a succession of results such, perhaps, as indicated in Fig. 316. In this example we have rows of isolated squares in white which may be turned hither and thither at pleasure, within certain angles, but they result in nothing more than monotonous successions of squares.

FIG. 318. Pattern produced by simple alternations of light and dark fillets. Basketry of the Indians of British Guiana.

Additional facility of expression is obtained by employing dark strands in the vertical series also, and large, isolated areas of solid color may be produced by changing the order of intersection, certain of the fillets being carried over two or more of the opposing series and in contiguous spaces at one step, as seen in Fig. 317. With these elementary resources the weaver has very considerable powers of expression, as will be seen in Fig. 318, which is taken from a basket made by South American Indians, and in Fig. 341, where human figures are delineated. The patterns in such cases are all rigidly geometric and exhibit stepped outlines of a pronounced kind. With impacting and increased refinement of fillets the stepped character is in a considerable measure lost sight of and realistic, graphic representation is to a greater extent within the workman's reach. It is probable, however, that the idea of weaving complex ideographic characters would not occur to the primitive mind at a very early date, and a long period of progress would elapse before delineative subjects would be attempted.

I do not need to follow this style of combination into the more refined kinds of work and into loom products, but may add that through all, until perverted by ulterior influences, the characteristic geometricity and monotonous repetition are allpervading.

For the purpose of looking still more closely into the tendencies of normal textile decorative development I shall present a series of Indian baskets, choosing mainly from the closely woven or impacted varieties because they are so well represented in our collections and at the same time are so very generally embellished with designs in color; besides, they are probably among the most simple and primitive textile products known. I have already shown that several types of combination when closely impacted produce very similar surface characters and encourage the same general style of decoration. In nearly all, the color features are confined to one series of fillets—those of the woof—the other, the warp, being completely hidden from view. In the preceding series the warp and woof were almost equally concerned in the expression of design. Here but one is used, and in consequence there is much freedom of expression, as the artist carries the colored filaments back and forth or inserts new ones at will. Still it will be seen that in doing this he is by no means free; he must follow the straight and narrow pathway laid down by the warp and woof, and, do what he may, he arrives at purely geometric results.

FIG. 319. Base of coiled basket showing the method of building by dual coiling. The base or warp coil is composed of untwisted fiber and is formed by adding to the free end as the coiling goes on. The woof or binding filament, as it is coiled, is caught into the upper surface of the preceding turn—1/8.

FIG. 320. Coiled basket with simple geometric ornament. Work of the northwest coast Indians—1/8.

I will now present the examples, which for the sake of uniformity are in all cases of the coiled ware. If a basket is made with no other idea than that of use the surface is apt to be pretty uniform in color, the natural color of the woof fillets. If decoration is desired a colored fillet is introduced, which, for the time, takes the place and does the duty of the ordinary strand. Fig. 319 serves to show the construction and surface appearance of the base of a coil made vessel still quite free from any color decoration. Now, if it is desired to begin a design, the plain wrapping thread is dropped and a colored fillet is inserted and the coiling continues. Carried once around the vessel we have an encircling line of dark color corresponding to the lower line of the ornament seen in Fig. 320. If the artist is content with a single line of color he sets the end of the dark thread and takes up the light colored one previously dropped and continues the coiling. If further elaboration is desired it is easily accomplished. In the example given the workman has taken up the dark fillet again and carried it a few times around the next turn of the warp coil; then it has been dropped and the white thread taken up, and again, in turn, another dark thread has been introduced and coiled for a few turns, and so on until four encircling rows of dark, alternating rectangles have been produced. Desiring to introduce a meandered design he has taken the upper series of rectangles as bases and adding colored filaments at the proper time has carried oblique lines, one to the right and the other to the left, across the six succeeding ridges of the warp coil. The pairs of stepped lines meeting above were joined in rectangles like those below, and the decoration was closed by a border line at the top. The vessel was then completed in the light colored material. In this ornament all forms are bounded by two classes of lines, vertical and horizontal (or, viewed from above or below, radial and encircling), the lines of the warp and the woof. Oblique bands of color are made up of series of rectangles, giving stepped outlines. Although these figures are purely geometric, it is not impossible that in their position and grouping they preserve a trace of some imitative conception modified to this shape by the forces of the art. They serve quite as well, however, to illustrate simple mechanical elaboration as if entirely free from suspicion of associated ideas.

FIG. 321. Coiled basket with encircling bands of ornament in white, red, and black, upon a yellowish ground. Obtained from the Indians of the Tule River, California—1/8.

In Fig. 321 I present a superb piece of work executed by the Indians of the Tule River, California. It is woven in the closely impacted, coiled style. The ornament is arranged in horizontal zones and consists of a series of diamond shaped figures in white with red centers and black frames set side by side. The processes of substitution where changes of color are required are the same as in the preceding case and the forms of figures and the disposition of designs are the same, being governed by the same forces.

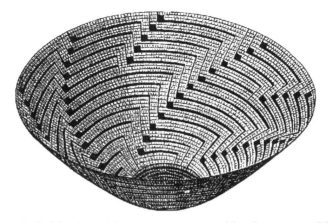

FIG. 322. Coiled basket with ornament arranged in zigzag rays. Obtained from the Pima Indians of Arizona—1/8.

Another choice piece, from the Pima Indians of Arizona, is given in Fig. 322. The lines of the ornament adhere exclusively to the directions imposed by the warp and the woof, the stripes of black color ascending with the turns of the fillet for a short distance, then for a time following the horizontal ridges, and again ascending, the complete result being a series of zigzag rays set very close together. These rays take an oblique turn to the left, and the dark figures at the angles, from the necessities of construction, form rows at right angles to these. A few supplementary rays are added toward the margin to fill out the widening spaces. Another striking example of the domination of technique over design is illustrated in Fig. 323.

FIG. 323. Coiled basket with two bands of meandered ornament. Obtained from the Pima Indians of Arizona—1/4.

Two strongly marked, fret-like meanders encircle the vessel, the elements of which are ruled exclusively by the warp and woof, by the radiate and the concentric lines of construction. This is the work of the Pima Indians of Arizona.

FIG. 324. Coiled basket with geometric ornament composed of triangular figures. Obtained from the McCloud River Indians, California—1/8.

I shall close the series with a very handsome example of Indian basketry and of basketry ornamentation (Fig. 324). The conical shape is highly pleasing and the design is thoroughly satisfactory and, like all the others, is applied in a way indicative of a refined sense of the decorative requirements of the utensil. The design is wholly geometric, and, although varied in appearance, is composed almost exclusively of dark triangular figures upon a light ground. The general grouping is in three horizontal or encircling bands agreeing with or following the foundation coil. Details are governed by the horizontal and the oblique structure lines. The vertical construction lines have no direct part in the conformation of the design excepting in so far as they impose a stepped character upon all oblique outlines.

These studies could be carried through all the types of primitive textile combination, but such a work seems unnecessary, for in all cases the elaboration in design, relieved and colored, is along similar lines, is governed by the same class of forces, and reaches closely corresponding results.

We have observed throughout the series of examples presented a decided tendency toward banded or zonal arrangement of the ornamentation. Now each of these bands is made up of a number of units, uniform in shape and in size and joined or linked together in various suitable and consistent ways. In contemplating them we are led to inquire into the nature of the forces concerned in the accomplishment of such results. The question arises as to exactly how much of the segregating and aggregating forces or tendencies belongs to the technique of the art and how much to the direct esthetic supervision of the human agent, questions as to ideographic influence being for the present omitted. This is a difficult problem to deal with, and I shall not attempt more here than to point out the apparent teachings of the examples studied.

The desires of the mind constitute the motive power, the force that gives rise to all progress in art; the appreciation of beauty and the desire to increase it are the cause of all progress in purely decorative elaboration. It appears, however, that there is in the mind no preconceived idea of what that elaboration should be. The mind is a growing thing and is led forward along the pathways laid out by environment. Seeking in art gratification of an esthetic kind it follows the lead of technique along the channels opened by such of the useful arts as offer suggestions of embellishment. The results reached vary with the arts and are important in proportion to the facilities furnished by the arts. As I have already amply shown, the textile art possesses vast advantages over all other arts in this respect, as it is first in the field, of widest application, full of suggestions of embellishment, and inexorably fixed in its methods of expression. The mind in its primitive, mobile condition is as clay in the grasp of technique.

A close analysis of the forces and the influences inherent in the art will be instructive. For the sake of simplicity I exclude from consideration all but purely mechanical or non-ideographic elements. It will be observed that order, uniformity, symmetry, are among the first lessons of the textile art. From the very beginning the workman finds it necessary to direct his attention to these considerations in the preparation of his material as well as in the building of his utensils. If parts employed in construction are multiple they must be uniform, and to reach definite results (presupposing always a demand for such results), either in form or ornament, there must be a constant counting of numbers and adjusting to spaces. The most fundamental and constant elements embodied in textile art and available for the expression of embellishment are the minute steps of the intersections or bindings; the most necessary and constant combination of these elements is in continuous lines or in rows of isolated figures; the most necessary and constant directions for these combinations are with the web and the woof, or with their complementaries, the diagonals. If large areas are covered certain separation or aggregation of the elements into larger units is called for, as otherwise absolute sameness would result. Such separation or aggregation conforms to the construction lines of the fabric, as any other arrangement would be unnatural and difficult of accomplishment. When the elements or units combine in continuous zones, bands, or rays they are placed side by side in simple juxtaposition or are united in various ways, always following the guide lines of construction through simple and complex convolutions. Whatever is done is at the suggestion of technique; whatever is done takes a form and arrangement imposed by technique. Results are like in like techniques and are unlike in unlike techniques; they therefore vary with the art and with its variations in time and character.

All those agencies pertaining to man that might be supposed important in this connection—the muscles of the hand and of the eye, the cell structure of the brain, together with all preconceived ideas of the beautiful—are all but impotent in the presence of technique, and, so far as forms of expression go, submit completely to its dictates. Ideas of the beautiful in linear geometric forms are actually formed by technique, and taste in selecting as the most beautiful certain ornaments produced in art is but choosing between products that in their evolution gave it its character and powers, precisely as the animal selects its favorite foods from among the products that throughout its history constitute its sustenance and shape its appetites.

Now, as primitive peoples advance from savagery to barbarism there comes a time in the history of all kinds of textile products at which the natural technical progress of decorative elaboration is interfered with by forces from without the art. This occurs when ideas, symbolic or otherwise, come to be associated with the purely geometric figures, tending to arrest or modify their development, or, again, it occurs when the artist seeks to substitute mythologic subjects for the geometric units. This period cannot be always well defined, as the first steps in this direction are so thoroughly subordinated to the textile forces. Between what may be regarded as purely technical, geometric ornament and ornament recognizably delineative, we find in each group of advanced textile products a series of forms of mixed or uncertain pedigree. These must receive slight attention here.

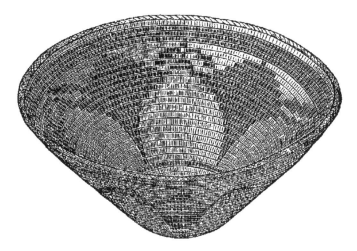

FIG. 325. Coiled basket ornamented with devices probably very highly conventionalized mythological subjects. Obtained from the Apache—1/8.

Fig. 325 represents a large and handsome basket obtained from the Apache. It will be seen that the outline of the figures comprising the principal zone of ornament departs somewhat from the four ruling directions of the textile combination. This was accomplished by increasing the width of the steps in the outline as the dark rays progressed, resulting in curved outlines of eccentric character. This eccentricity, coupled with the very unusual character of the details at the outer extremities of the figures, leads to the surmise that each part of the design is a conventional representation of some life form, a bird, an insect, or perhaps a man.

By the free introduction of such elements textile ornament loses its pristine geometric purity and becomes in a measure degraded. In the more advanced stages of Pueblo art the ornament of nearly all the textiles is pervaded by ideographic characters, generally rude suggestions of life forms, borrowed, perhaps, from mythologic art. This is true of much of the coiled basketry of the Moki Indians. True, many examples occur in which the ancient or indigenous geometric style is preserved, but the majority appear to be more or less modified. In many cases nothing can be learned from a study of the designs themselves, as the particular style of construction is not adapted to realistic expression, and, at best, resemblances to natural forms are very remote. Two examples are given in Figs. 326 and 327. I shall expect, however, when the art of these peoples is better known, to learn to what particular mythic concept these mixed or impure geometric devices refer.

FIG. 326. Coiled tray with geometric devices probably modified by ideographic association. Moki work—1/4.

The same is true of other varieties of Pueblo basketry, notably the common decorated wickerware, two specimens of which are given in Figs. 328 and 329. This ware is of the interlaced style, with radially arranged web filaments. Its geometric characters are easily distinguished from those of the coiled ware. Many examples exhibit purely conventional elaboration, the figures being arranged in rays, zones, checkers, and the like. It is to be expected, however, that the normal ornament of this class of products should be greatly interfered with through attempts to introduce extraneous elements, for the peoples have advanced to a stage of culture at which it is usual to attempt the introduction of mythologic representations into all art. Further consideration of this subject will be necessary in the next section of this paper.

FIG. 327. Coiled tray with geometric devices, probably modified by ideographic association. Moki work—1/4.

FIG. 328. Tray of interlaced style of weaving, showing geometric ornament, probably modified by ideographic association. Moki work—1/4.

The processes of pure geometric elaboration with which this section is mainly concerned can be studied to best advantage in more primitive forms of art.

FIG. 329. Tray of interlaced style of weaving, showing geometric ornament, probably modified by ideographic association. Moki work—1/4.

Non-essential constructive features.—Now, all the varied effects of color and design described in the preceding paragraphs are obtained without seriously modifying the simple necessary construction, without resorting to the multiple extraordinary devices within easy reach. The development and utilization of the latter class of resources must now receive attention. In the preceding examples, when it was desired to begin a figure in color the normal ground filament was dropped out and a colored one set into its place and made to fill its office while it remained; but we find that in many classes of work the colored elements were added to the essential parts, not substituted for them, although they are usually of use in perfecting the fabric by adding to serviceability as well as to beauty. This is illustrated, for example, by the doubling of one series or of both warp and woof, by the introduction of pile, by wrapping filaments with strands of other colors, or by twisting in feathers. Savage nations in all parts of the world are acquainted with devices of this class and employ them with great freedom. The effects produced often correspond closely to needlework, and the materials employed are often identical in both varieties of execution.

The following examples will serve to illustrate my meaning. The effect seen in Fig. 330 is observed in a small hand wallet obtained in Mexico. The fillets employed appear to be wide, flattened straws of varied colors. In order to avoid the monotony of a plain checker certain of the light fillets are wrapped with thin fillets of dark tint in such a way that when woven the dark color appears in small squares placed diagonally with the fundamental checkers. Additional effects are produced by covering certain portions of the filaments with straws of distinct color, all being woven in with the fabric. By other devices certain parts of the fillets are made to stand out from the surface in sharp points and in ridges, forming geometric figures, either normal or added elements being employed. Another device is shown in Fig. 331. Here a pattern is secured by carrying dark fillets back and forth over the light colored fabric, catching them down at regular intervals during the process of weaving. Again, feathers and other embellishing media are woven in with the woof. Two interesting baskets procured from the Indians of the northwest coast are shown in Figs. 332 and 333. Feathers of brilliant hues are fixed to and woven in with certain of the woof strands, which are treated, in the execution of patterns, just as are ordinary colored threads, care being taken not to destroy the beauty of the feathers in the process. The richly colored feathers lying smoothly in one direction are made to represent various figures necessarily geometric. This simple work is much surpassed, however, by the marvelous feather ornamentation of the Mexicans and Peruvians, of which glowing accounts are given by historians and of which a few meager traces are found in tombs. Much of the feather work of all nations is of the nature of embroidery and will receive attention further on. A very clever device practiced by the northwest coast tribes consists in the use of two woof strands of contrasting colors, one or the other being made to appear on the surface, as the pattern demands.

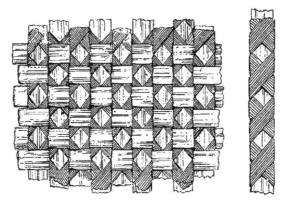

FIG. 330. Ornament produced by wrapping certain light fillets with darker ones before weaving. Mexican work.

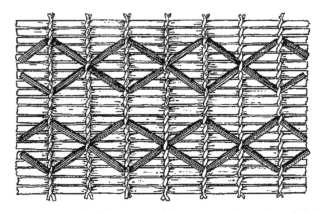

FIG. 331. Ornamental effect secured by weaving in series of dark fillets, forming a superficial device. Work of the Klamath Indians.

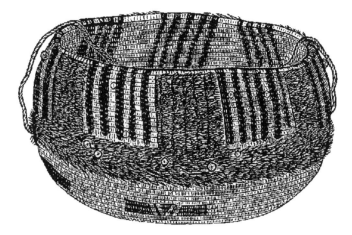

FIG. 332. Baskets ornamented with feather work. Northwest coast tribes—1/4.

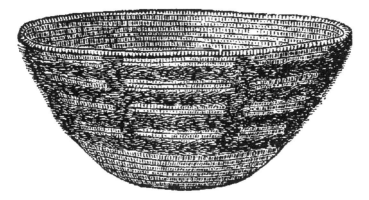

FIG. 333. Baskets ornamented with feather work. Northwest coast tribes—1/4.

An example from a higher grade of art will be of value in this connection. The ancient Peruvians resorted to many clever devices for purposes of enrichment. An illustration of the use of extra-constructional means to secure desired ends are given in Figs. 334 and 335. Threads constituting a supplemental warp and woof are carried across the under side of a common piece of fabric, that they may be brought up and woven in here and there to produce figures of contrasting color upon the right side. Fig. 334 shows the right side of the cloth, with the secondary series appearing in the border and central figure only. Fig. 335 illustrates the opposite side and shows the loose hanging, unused portions of the auxiliary series. In such work, when the figures are numerous and occupy a large part of the surface, the fabric is really a double one, having a dual warp and woof. Examples could be multiplied indefinitely, but it will readily be seen from what has been presented that the results of these extraordinary means cannot differ greatly from those legitimately produced by the fundamental filaments alone.

FIG. 334. Piece of cotton cloth showing the use of a supplementary web and woof. Ancient Peru.

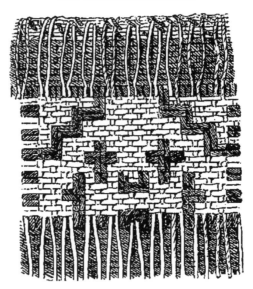

FIG. 335. Piece of cotton cloth showing the use of a supplementary web and woof. Ancient Peru.

Superconstructive features.—In reviewing the superconstructive decorative features in the preceding section I classified them somewhat closely by method of execution or application to the fabric, as stitched, inserted, drawn, cut, applied, and appended. It will be seen that, although these devices are to a great extent of the nature of needlework, all cannot be classed under this head.

Before needles came into use the decorative features were inserted and attached in a variety of ways. In open work nothing was needed but the end of the fillet or part inserted; again, in close work, perforations were made as in leather work, and the threads were inserted as are the waxed ends of the shoemaker.

The importance of this class of decorative devices to primitive peoples will be apparent if we but call to mind the work of our own Indian tribes. What a vast deal of attention is paid to those classes of embroideries in which beads, feathers, quills, shells, seeds, teeth, &c., are employed, and to the multitude of novel applications of tassels, fringes, and tinkling pendants. The taste for these things is universal and their relation to the development of esthetic ideas is doubtless very intimate.

Needlework arose in the earliest stages of art and at first was employed in joining parts, such as leaves, skins, and tissues, for various useful purposes, and afterwards in attaching ornaments. In time the attaching media, as exposed in stitches, loops, knots, and the like, being of bright colors, were themselves utilized as embellishment, and margins and apertures were beautified by various bindings and borders, and finally patterns were worked in contrasting colors upon the surfaces of the cloths and other materials of like nature or use.

No other art so constantly and decidedly suggested embellishment and called for the exercise of taste. It was the natural habitat for decoration. It was the field in which technique and taste were most frequently called upon to work hand in hand.

With the growth of culture the art was expanded and perfected, its wonderful capacity for expression leading from mere bindings to pretentious borders, to patterns, to the introduction of ideographs, to the representation of symbols and mythologic subjects, and from these to the delineation of nature, the presentation of historical and purely pictorial scenes.

And now a few words in regard to the character of the work and its bearing upon the geometric system of decoration. As purely constructive ornamentation has already been presented, I will first take up that class of superconstructive work most nearly related to it. In some varieties of basketry certain bindings of the warp and woof are actually left imperfect, with the idea of completing the construction by subsequent processes, the intersections being gone over stitch by stitch and lashed together, the embroidery threads passing in regular order through the openings of the mesh. This process is extremely convenient to the decorator, as changes from one color to another are made without interfering with construction, and the result is of a closely similar character to that reached by working the colors in with warp and woof. In a very close fabric this method cannot be employed, but like results are reached by passing the added filaments beneath the protruding parts of the bindings and, stitch by stitch, covering up the plain fabric, working bright patterns. Fig. 336 is intended to show how this is done. The foundation is of twined work and the decorating fillets are passed under by lifting, with or without a needle. This process is extensively practiced by our west coast tribes, and the results are extremely pleasing. The materials most used are quills and bright colored straws, the foundation fabric being of bark or of rushes. The results in such work are generally geometric, in a way corresponding more or less closely with the ground work combination.

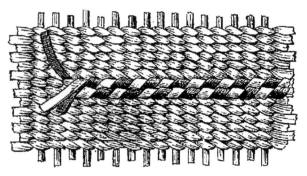

FIG. 336. Grass embroidery upon the surface of closely impacted, twined basketry. Work of the northwest coast Indians.

A large class of embroideries are applied by like processes, but without reference to the construction of the foundation fabric, as they are also applied to felt and leather. Again, artificially prepared perforations are used, through which the fillets are passed. The results are much less uniformly geometric than where the fabric is followed; yet the mere adding of the figures, stitch by stitch or part by part, is sufficient to impart a large share of geometricity, as may be seen in the buckskin bead work and in the dentalium and quill work of the Indians.

Feather embroidery was carried to a high degree of perfection by our ancient aborigines, and the results were perhaps the most brilliant of all these wonderful decorations. I have already shown how feathers are woven in with the warp and woof, and may now give a single illustration of the application of feather work to the surfaces of fabrics. Among the beautiful articles recovered from the tombs of Ancon, Peru, are some much decayed specimens of feather work. In our example delicate feathers of red, blue, and yellow hues are applied to the surface of a coarse cotton fabric by first carefully tying them together in rows at regular distances and afterwards stitching them down, as shown in Fig. 337.

The same method is practiced by modern peoples in many parts of the world. Other decorative materials are applied in similar ways by attachment to cords or fillets which are afterwards stitched down. In all this work the geometricity is entirely or nearly uniform with that of the foundation fabrics. Other classes of decoration, drawn work, appliqué, and the like, are not of great importance in aboriginal art and need no additional attention here, as they have but slight bearing upon the development of design.

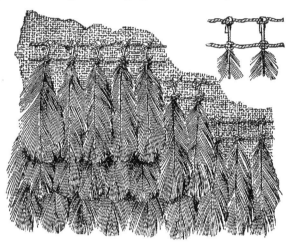

FIG. 337. Feather embroidery of the ancient Peruvians, showing the method of attaching the feathers.

Attached or appended ornaments constitute a most important part of decorative resource. They are less subject to the laws of geometricity, being fixed to surfaces and margins without close reference to the web and woof. They include fringes, tassels, and the multitude of appendable objects, natural and artificial, with which primitive races bedeck their garments and utensils. A somewhat detailed study of this class of ornament is given at the end of the preceding section.

Adventitious features.—Ornament is applied to the surfaces of fabrics by painting and by stamping. These methods of decoration were employed in very early times and probably originated in other branches of art. If the surface features of the textile upon which a design is painted are strongly pronounced, the figures produced with the brush or pencil will tend to follow them, giving a decidedly geometric result. If the surface is smooth the hand is free to follow its natural tendencies, and the results will be analogous in character to designs painted upon pottery, rocks, or skins. In primitive times both the texture of the textiles and the habits of the decorator, acquired in textile work, tended towards the geometric style of delineation, and we find that in work in which the fabric lines are not followed at all the designs are still geometric, and geometric in the same way as are similar designs woven in with the fabric. Illustrations of this are given in the next section.

I have dwelt at sufficient length upon the character and the tendencies of the peculiar system of embellishment that arises within textile art as the necessary outgrowth of technique, and now proceed to explain the relations of this system to associated art.

In the strong forward tendency of the textile system of decoration it has made two conquests of especial importance. In the first place it has subdued and assimilated all those elements of ornament that have happened to enter its realm from without, and in the second place it has imposed its habits and customs upon the decorative systems of all arts with which the textile art has come in contact.

GEOMETRICITY IMPOSED UPON ADOPTED ELEMENTS OF DESIGN.

At a very early stage of culture most peoples manifest decided artistic tendencies, which are revealed in attempts to depict various devices, life forms, and fancies upon the skin and upon the surfaces of utensils, garments, and other articles and objects. The figures are very often decorative in effect and may be of a trivial nature, but very generally such art is serious and pertains to events or superstitions. The devices employed may be purely conventional or geometric, containing no graphic element whatever; but life forms afford the most natural and satisfactory means of recording, conveying, and symbolizing ideas, and hence preponderate largely. Such forms, on account of their intimate relations with the philosophy of the people, are freely embodied in every art suitable to their employment. As already seen, the peculiar character of textile construction places great difficulties in the way of introducing unsymmetric and complex figures like those of natural objects into fabrics. The idea of so employing them may originally have been suggested by the application of designs in color to the woven surfaces or by resemblances between the simpler conventional life form derivatives and the geometric figures indigenous to the art.

At any rate, the idea of introducing life forms into the texture was suggested, and in the course of time a great deal of skill was shown in their delineation, the bolder workmen venturing to employ a wide range of graphic subjects.

Now, if we examine these woven forms with reference to the modifications brought about by the textile surveillance, we find that the figures, as introduced in the cloth, do not at all correspond with those executed by ordinary graphic methods, either in degree of elaboration or in truthfulness of expression. They have a style of their own. Each delineative element upon entering the textile realm is forced into those peculiar conventional outlines imposed by the geometric construction, the character of which has already been dwelt upon at considerable length. We find, however, that the degree of convention is not uniform throughout all fabrics, but that it varies with the refinement of the threads or filaments, the compactness of the mesh, the character of the combination, the graphic skill of the artist, and the tendencies of his mind; yet we observe that through all there is still exhibited a distinct and peculiar geometricity.

So pronounced is this technical bias that delineations of a particular creature—as, for example, a bird—executed by distant and unrelated peoples, are reduced in corresponding styles of fabric to almost identical shapes. This conventionalizing force is further illustrated by the tendency in textile representation to blot out differences of time and culture, so that when a civilized artisan, capable of realistic pictorial delineation of a high order, introduces a figure into a certain form of coarse fabric he arrives at a result almost identical with that reached by the savage using the same, who has no graphic language beyond the rudest outline.

A number of examples may be given illustrating this remarkable power of textile combination over ornament. I select three in which the human figure is presented. One is chosen from Iroquoian art, one from Digger Indian art, and one from the art of the Incas—peoples unequal in grade of culture, isolated geographically, and racially distinct. I have selected specimens in which the parts employed give features of corresponding size, so that comparisons are easily instituted. The example shown in Fig. 338 illustrates a construction peculiar to the wampum belts of the Iroquois and their neighbors, and quite unlike ordinary weaving. It is taken from the middle portion of what is known as the Penn wampum belt. The horizontal series of strands consists of narrow strips of buckskin, through which the opposing series of threads are sewed, holding in place the rows of cylindrical shell beads. Purple beads are employed to develop the figures in a ground of white beads. If the maker of this belt had been required to execute in chalk a drawing depicting brotherly love the results would have been very different.

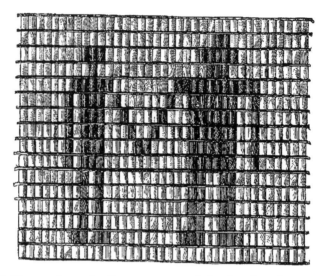

FIG. 338. Figures from the Penn wampum belt, showing the conventional form imposed in bead work.

My second illustration (Fig. 339) is drawn from a superb example of the basketry of the Yokut Indians of California. The two figures form part of a spirally radiating band of ornament, which is shown to good advantage in the small cut. Fig. 340. It is of the coiled style of construction. The design is worked in four colors and the effect is quiet and rich.

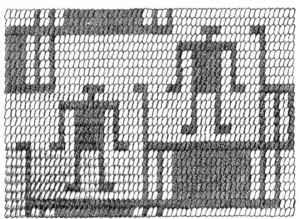

FIG. 339. Conventional figures from a California Indian basket.

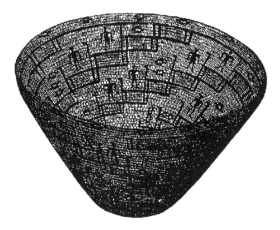

FIG. 340. Basket made by the Yokut Indians of California.

Turning southward from California and passing through many strange lands we find ourselves in Peru, and among a class of remains that bespeak a high grade of culture. The inhabitants of Ancon were wonderfully skilled in the textile art, and thousands of handsome examples have been obtained from their ancient tombs. Among these relics are many neat little workbaskets woven from rushes. One of these, now in the National Museum, is encircled by a decorated belt in which are represented seven human figures woven in black filaments upon a brown ground.

The base and rim of the basket are woven in the intertwined combination, but in the decorated belt the style is changed to the plain right angled interlacing, for the reason, no doubt, that this combination was better suited to the development of the intended design. Besides the fundamental series of fillets the weaver resorted to unusual devices in order to secure certain desired results. In the first place the black horizontal series of filaments does not alternate in the simplest way with the brown series, but, where a wide space of the dark color is called for, several of the brown strands are passed over at one step, as in the head and body, and in the wider interspaces the dark strands pass under two or more of the opposing strands. In this way broad areas of color are obtained. It will be observed, however, that the construction is weakened by this modification, and that to remedy the defect two additional extra constructive series of fillets are added. These are of much lighter weight than the main series, that they may not obscure the pattern. Over the dark series they run vertically and over the light obliquely.

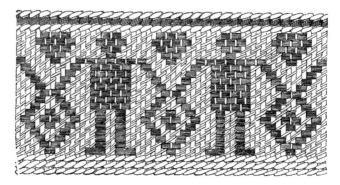

FIG. 341. Conventional human figures from an ancient Peruvian basket.

It will be seen that the result, notwithstanding all this modification of procedure, is still remarkably like that of the preceding examples, the figures corresponding closely in kind and degree of geometricity.

The fact is that in this coarse work refinement of drawing is absolutely unattainable. It appears that the sharply pronounced steps exhibited in the outlines are due to the great width of the fillets used. With the finer threads employed by most nations of moderate culture the stepped effect need not obtrude itself, for smooth outlines and graceful curves are easily attainable; yet, as a rule, even the finer fabrics continue to exhibit in their decorations the pronounced geometric character seen in ruder forms. I present a striking example of this in Fig. 342, a superb piece of Incarian gobelins, in which a gaily costumed personage is worked upon a dark red ground dotted with symbols and strange devices. The work is executed in brilliant colors and in great detail. But with all the facility afforded for the expression of minutely modulated form the straight lines and sharp angles are still present. The traditions of the art were favorable to great geometricity, and the tendencies of the warp and woof and the shape of the spaces to be filled were decidedly in that direction.

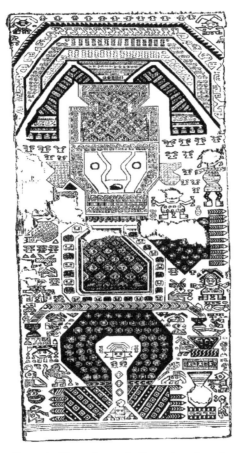

FIG. 342. Human figure in Peruvian gobelins, showing characteristic textile convention. From chromolithographs published by Reiss and Stübel in The Necropolis of Ancon.

FIG. 343. Human figures from a Peruvian vase, done in free hand, graphic style.

In order that the full force of my remarks may be appreciable to the eye of the reader, I give an additional illustration (Fig. 343). The two figures here shown, although I am not able to say positively that the work is pre-Columbian, were executed by a native artist of about the same stage of culture as was the work of the textile design. These figures are executed in color upon the smooth surface of an earthen vase and illustrate perfectly the peculiar characters of free hand, graphic delineation. Place this and the last figure side by side and we see how vastly different is the work of two artists of equal capacity when executed in the two methods. This figure should also be compared with the embroidered figures shown in Fig. 348.

The tendencies to uniformity in textile ornament here illustrated may be observed the world over. Every element entering the art must undergo a similar metamorphosis; hence the remarkable power of this almost universally practiced art upon the whole body of decorative design.

FIG. 344. Human figure modified by execution in concentric interlaced style of weaving—1/3.

That the range of results produced by varying styles of weaving and of woven objects may be appreciated, I present some additional examples. Coiled wares, for instance, present decorative phenomena strikingly at variance with those in which there is a rectangular disposition of parts. Instead of the two or more interlacing series of parallel fillets exhibited in the latter style, we have one radiate and one concentric series. The effect of this arrangement upon the introduced human figure is very striking, as will be seen by reference to Fig. 344, which represents a large tray obtained from the Moki Indians. The figure probably represents one of the mythologic personages of the Moki pantheon or some otherwise important priestly functionary, wearing the characteristic headdress of the ceremony in which the plaque was to be used. The work is executed in wicker, stained in such bright tints as were considered appropriate to the various features of the costume. Referring in detail to the shape and arrangement of the parts of the figure, it is apparent that many of the remarkable features are due to constructive peculiarities. The round face, for example, does not refer to the sun or the moon, but results from the concentric weaving. The oblique eyes have no reference to a Mongolian origin, as they only follow the direction of the ray upon which they are woven, and the headdress does not refer to the rainbow or the aurora because it is arched, but is arched because the construction forced it into this shape. The proportion of the figure is not so very bad because the Moki artist did not know better, but because the surface of the tray did not afford room to project the body and limbs.

FIG. 345. Figure of a bird painted upon a Zuñi shield, free hand delineation.

Now, it may be further observed that had the figure been placed at one side of the center, extending only from the border to the middle of the tray, an entirely different result would have been reached; but this is better illustrated in a series of bird delineations presented in the following figures. With many tribes the bird is an object of superstitious interest and is introduced freely into all art products suitable for its delineation. It is drawn upon walls, skins, pottery, and various utensils and weapons, especially those directly connected with ceremonies in which the mythical bird is an important factor. The bird form was probably in familiar use long before it was employed in the decoration of basketry. In Fig. 345 I present an ordinary graphic representation. It is copied from a Zuñi shield and is the device of an order or the totem of a clan. The style is quite conventional, as a result of the various constraints surrounding its production. But what a strange metamorphosis takes place when it is presented in the basketmaker's language. Observe the conventional pattern shown upon the surface of a Moki tray (Fig. 346). We have difficulty in recognizing the bird at all, although the conception is identical with the preceding. The positions of the head and legs and the expanded wings and tail correspond as closely as possible, but delineation is hampered by technique. The peculiar construction barely permits the presentation of a recognizable life form, and permits it in a particular way, which will be understood by a comparison with the treatment of the human figure in Fig. 344. In that case the interlaced combination gives relievo results, characterized by wide, radiating ribs and narrow, inconspicuous, concentric lines, which cross the ribs in long steps. The power of expression lies almost wholly with the concentric series, and detail must in a great measure follow the concentric lines. In the present case (Fig. 346) this is reversed and lines employed in expressing forms are radiate.

FIG. 346. Figure of a bird executed in a coiled Moki tray, textile delineation.

The precise effect of this difference of construction upon a particular feature may be shown by the introduction of another illustration. In Fig. 347 we have a bird woven in a basket of the interlaced style. We see with what ease the long sharp bill and the slender tongue (shown by a red filament between the two dark mandibles) are expressed. In the other case the construction is such that the bill, if extended in the normal direction, is broad and square at the end, and the tongue, instead of lying between the mandibles, must run across the bill, totally at variance with the truth; in this case the tongue is so represented, the light vertical band seen in the cut being a yellow stripe. It will be seen that the two representations are very unlike each other, not because of differences in the conception and not wholly on account of the style of weaving, but rather because the artist chose to extend one across the whole surface of the utensil and to confine the other to one side of the center.

FIG. 347. Figure of a bird woven in interlaced wicker at one side of the center.

It is clear, therefore, from the preceding observations that the convention of woven life forms varies with the kind of weaving, with the shape of the object, with the position upon the object, and with the shape of the space occupied, as well as with the inherited style of treatment and with the capacity of the artist concerned. These varied forces and influences unite in the metamorphosis of all the incoming elements of textile embellishment.

It will be of interest to examine somewhat closely the modifications produced in pictorial motives introduced through superstructural and adventitious agencies.

We are accustomed, at this age of the world, to see needlework employed successfully in the delineation of graphic forms and observe that even the Indian, under the tutelage of the European, reproduces in a more or less realistic way the forms of vegetal and animal life. As a result we find it difficult to realize the simplicity and conservatism of primitive art. The intention of the primitive artist was generally not to depict nature, but to express an idea or decorate a space, and there was no strong reason why the figures should not submit to the conventionalizing tendencies of the art.

I have already shown that embroidered designs, although not from necessity confined to geometric outlines, tend to take a purely geometric character from the fabric upon which they are executed, as well as from the mechanical processes of stitching. This is well shown in Fig. 348, a fine specimen given by Wiener in his work Pérou et Bolive.

FIG. 348. Embroidery upon a cotton net in which the textile combinations are followed step by step. Ancient Peruvian work.

A life form worked upon a net does not differ essentially from the same subject woven in with the web and woof. The reason is found in the fact that in embroidery the workman was accustomed from the first to follow the geometric combination of the foundation fabric step by step, and later in life delination he pursued the same method.

It would seem natural, however, that when the foundation fabric does not exhibit well marked geometric characters, as in compactly woven canvas, the needlework would assume free hand characters and follow the curves and irregularities of the natural object depicted; but such is not the case in purely aboriginal work. An example of embroidery obtained from an ancient grave at Ancon, Peru, is shown in Fig. 349. A piece of brown cotton canvas is embellished with a border of bird figures in bright colored wool thread. The lines of the figures do not obey the web and woof strictly, as the lines are difficult to follow, but the geometric character is as perfectly preserved as if the design were woven in the goods.

FIG. 349. Embroidery in which the foundation fabric is not followed accurately, but which exhibits the full textile geometricity. Ancient Peruvian work.

FIG. 350. Design painted in color upon a woven surface, exhibiting the full degree of geometric convention. Ancient Peruvian work. Copied from The Necropolis of Ancon.

So habit and association carry the geometric system into adventitious decoration. When the ancient Peruvian executed a design in color upon a woven surface (Fig. 350), using a pencil or brush, the result was hardly less subject to textile restraint.

As a matter of course, since there are two distinct styles of decorative design—the textile and the free hand—there exist intermediate forms partaking of the character of both; but it is nevertheless clear that the textile system transforms or greatly modifies all nature motives associated with it, whether introduced into the fabric or applied to its surface.

In countries where the textile art is unimportant and the textile system of decoration does not obtrude itself, free hand methods may prevail to such an extent that the geometric influence is but little felt. The Haidah Indians, for example, paint designs with great freedom and skill, and those applied to woven surfaces are identical with those executed upon skins, wood, and stone, but this art is doubtless much modified by the means and methods of Europeans. Our studies should be confined wholly to pure indigenous art.

EXTENSION OF TEXTILE ORNAMENT TO OTHER FORMS OF ART.

I have now dwelt at sufficient length upon the character of the textile system of ornament and have laid especial stress upon the manner in which it is interwoven with the technical constitution of the art. I have illustrated the remarkable power of the art by which decorative elements from without, coming once within the magic influence, are seized upon and remodeled in accordance with the laws of textile combination. Pursuing the investigation still further it is found that the dominion of the textile system is not limited to the art, but extends to other arts. Like a strong race of men it is not to be confined to its own original habitat, but spreads to other realms, stamping its own habits and character upon whatever happens to come within its reach. Its influence is felt throughout the whole range of those arts with which the esthetic sense of man seeks to associate ideas of beauty. It is necessary, before closing this paper, to examine briefly the character and extent of this influence and to describe in some detail the agencies through which the results are accomplished. First and most important are the results of direct transmission.

House building, or architecture as it is called in the higher stages, is in primitive times to a great extent textile; as culture develops, other materials and other systems of construction are employed, and the resultant forms vary accordingly; but textile characters are especially strong and persistent in the matter of ornament, and survive all changes, howsoever complete. In a similar way other branches of art differentiated in material and function from the parent art inherit many characters of form and ornament conceived in the textile stage. It may be difficult to say with reference to any particular example of design that it had a textile origin, for there may be multiple origins to the same or to closely corresponding forms; but we may assert in a general way of the great body of geometric ornament that it owes something—if not its inspiration, its modes of expression—to the teachings of the textile system. This appears reasonable when we consider that the weaver's art, as a medium of esthetic ideas, had precedence in time over nearly all competitors. Being first in the field it stood ready on the birth of new forms of art, whether directly related or not, to impose its characters upon them. What claim can architecture, sculpture, or ceramics have upon the decorative conceptions of the Digger Indians, or even upon those of the Zuñi or Moki? The former have no architecture, sculpture, or ceramics; but their system of decoration, as we have seen, is highly developed. The Pueblo tribes at their best have barely reached the stage at which esthetic ideas are associated with building; yet classic art has not produced a set of geometric motives more chaste or varied. These examples of the development of high forms of decoration during the very early stages of the arts are not isolated. Others are observed in other countries, and it is probable that if we could lift the veil and peer into the far prehistoric stages of the world's greatest cultures the same condition and order would be revealed. It is no doubt true that all of the shaping arts in the fullness of their development have given rise to decorative features peculiar to themselves; for construction, whether in stone, clay, wood, or metal, in their rigid conditions, exhibits characters unknown before, many of which tend to give rise to ornament. But this ornament is generally only applicable to the art in which it develops, and is not transferable by natural processes—as of a parent to its offspring—as are the esthetic features of the weaver's art.

Besides the direct transmission of characters and forms as suggested in a preceding paragraph, there are many less direct but still efficacious methods of transfer by means of which various arts acquire textile decorative features, as will be seen by the following illustrations.

Japanese art is celebrated for its exquisite decorative design. Upon superb works of porcelain we have skillful representations of subjects taken from nature and from mythology, which are set with perfect taste upon fields or within borders of elaborate geometric design. If we should ask how such motives came to be employed in ceramic decoration, the answer would be given that they were selected and employed because they were regarded as fitting and beautiful by a race of decorators whose taste is well nigh infallible. But this explanation, however satisfactory as applied to individual examples of modern art, is not at all applicable to primitive art, for the mind of man was not primarily conscious of the beauty or fitness of decorative elements, nor did he think of using them independently of the art to which they were indigenous. Now the ceramic art gives rise to comparatively few elements of decoration, and must therefore acquire the great body of its decorative motives from other arts by some process not primarily dependent upon the exercise of judgment or taste, and yet not by direct inheritance, as the techniques of the two arts are wholly distinct.

Textile and fictile arts are, in their earlier stages, to a large extent, vessel making arts, the one being functionally the offshoot of the other. The textile art is the parent, and, as I have already shown, develops within itself a geometric system of ornament. The fictile art is the offshoot and has within itself no predilection for decoration. It is dependent and plastic. Its forms are to a great extent modeled and molded within the textile shapes and acquire automatically some of the decorative surface characters of the mold. This is the beginning of the transfer, and as time goes on other methods are suggested by which elements indigenous to the one art are transferred to the other. Thus we explain the occurrence, the constant recurrence of certain primary decorative motives in primitive ceramics. The herring bone, the checker, the guilloche, and the like are greatly the heritage of the textile art. Two forms derived from textile surfaces are illustrated in Figs. 351 and 352. In the first example shown, herring bone patterns appear as the result of textile combination, and in the second a triangular checker is produced in the same way. In Fig. 352 we see the result of copying these patterns in incised lines upon soft clay.

FIG. 351. Herring bone and checker patterns produced in textile combinations.

FIG. 352. Herring bone and checker figures in fictile forms transferred from the textile.

Again, the ancient potter, who was in the habit of modeling his wares within baskets, seems to have conceived the idea of building his vessels by coiling just as he built his baskets. The surface exhibits coiled ridges like basketry, as shown in Fig. 353, and the textile character was further imposed upon the clay by marking these coils with the thumb and with implements to give the effect of the transverse series of filaments, and the geometric color patterns of the basketry were reproduced in incised lines. When these peoples came to paint their wares it was natural that the colored patterns native to the basketry should also be reproduced, and many more or less literal transfers by copying are to be found. A fine example of these painted textile designs is shown in Fig. 354. It is executed in a masterly style upon a handsome vase of the white ware of ancient Tusayan. Not only are the details reproduced with all their geometric exactness, but the arrangement of the designs upon the vessel is the same as in the textile original. Nine-tenths of the more archaic, Pueblo, ceramic, ornamental designs are traceable to the textile art, and all show the influence of textile convention.

FIG. 353. Earthen vase built by coiling, exhibiting decorative characters derived from basketry.

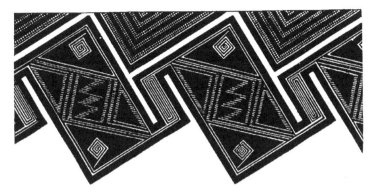

FIG. 354. Ceramic ornament copied literally from a textile original.

Another peculiar class of transfers of a somewhat more indirect nature may be noticed. All the more advanced American nations were very fond of modeling the human form in clay, a large percentage of vessels having some trace of the human form or physiognomy. Now, in many cases the costume of the personage represented in the clay is also imitated, and generally in color, the details of the fabrics receiving their full share of attention. Such an example, from a sepulcher at Ancon, is shown in Fig. 355. Here the poncho or mantle thrown across the shoulders falls down upon the body in front and behind and the stripes and conventional fishes are accurately reproduced. In this way both style and matter of the textile decoration are introduced into the ceramic art.

FIG. 355. Textile patterns transferred to pottery through the copying of costume. From The Necropolis of Ancon, by Reiss and Stübel, Pl. 94.

It will be seen by these illustrations that there are many natural methods, automatic or semiautomatic in character, by which the one art receives aid from the other; that in the beginning of the transfer of textile ornament to fictile forms the process is purely mechanical, and that it is continued automatically without any very decided exercise of judgment or taste. As a result, these borrowed decorations are generally quite as consistent and appropriate as if developed within the art itself. Later in the course of progress the potter escapes in a measure from this narrow groove and elaborates his designs with more freedom, being governed still to a certain extent by the laws of instinctive and automatic procedure. When, finally, intellect assumes to carry on the work independently of these laws, decoration tends to become debased.

Turning to other branches of art, what traces do we find of the transfer to them of textile features? Take, for example, sculpture. In the wood carving of the Polynesians we observe a most elaborate system of decoration, more or less geometric in character. We do not need to look a second time to discover a striking likeness to the textile system, and we ask, Is it also derived from a textile source? In the first place let us seek within the art a reason for the peculiar forms. In carving wood and in tracing figures upon it with pointed tools the tendency would certainly be towards straight lines and formal combinations; but in this work there would be a lack of uniformity in execution and of persistency in narrow lines of combination, such as result from the constant necessity of counting and spacing in the textile art. In the presentation of natural forms curved lines are called for, and there is nothing inherent in the carver's art to forbid the turning of such lines with the graver or knife. Graphic art would be realistic to an extent regulated by the skill and habits of the artist. But, in reality, the geometric character of this work is very pronounced, and we turn naturally toward the textile art to ask whether in some way that art has not exercised an influence. The textile arts of these peoples are highly developed and were doubtless so in a degree from very early times, and must have had a close relation with the various arts, and especially so in the matter of ornament. Specific examples may be cited showing the intimacy of wood carving to textilia. Bows, spears, arrows, &c. are bound with textile materials to increase their strength. Knives and other weapons are covered with textile sheaths and handles of certain utensils are lashed on with twisted cords. In ceremonial objects these textile features are elaborated for ornament and the characteristic features of this ornament are transferred to associated surfaces of wood and stone by the graver. A most instructive illustration is seen in the ceremonial adzes so numerous in museums (Fig. 356). The cords used primarily in attaching the haft are, after loss of function, elaborately plaited and interwoven until they become an important feature and assume the character of decoration. The heavy wooden handles are elaborately carved, and the suggestions of figures given by the interlaced cords are carried out in such detail that at a little distance it is impossible to say where the real textile surface ceases and the sculptured portion begins.

All things considered, I regard it as highly probable that much of the geometric character exhibited in Polynesian decoration is due to textile dominance. That these peoples are in the habit of employing textile designs in non-textile arts is shown in articles of costume, such as the tapa cloths, made from the bark of the mulberry tree, which are painted or stamped in elaborate geometric patterns. This transfer is also a perfectly natural one, as the ornament is applied to articles having functions identical with the woven stuffs in which the patterns originate, and, besides, the transfer is accomplished by means of stamps themselves textile. Fig. 357 illustrates the construction of these stamps and indicates just how the textile character is acquired.

FIG. 356. Ceremonial adz, with carved ornament imitating textile wrapping. Polynesian work.

Textile materials are very generally associated with the human figure in art, and thus sculpture, which deals chiefly with the human form, becomes familiar with geometric motives and acquires them. Through sculpture these motives enter architecture. But textile decoration pervades architecture before the sculptor's chisel begins to carve ornament in stone and before architecture has developed of itself the rudiments of a system of surface embellishment. Textile art in mats, covers, shelters, and draperies is intimately associated with floors and walls of houses, and the textile devices are in time transferred to the stone and plaster. The wall of an ancient Pueblo estufa, or ceremonial chamber, built in the pre-esthetic period of architecture, antedating, in stage of culture, the first known step in Egyptian art, is encircled by a band of painted figures, borrowed, like those of the pottery, from a textile source. The doorway or rather entrance to the rude hovel of a Navajo Indian is closed by a blanket of native make, unsurpassed in execution and exhibiting conventional designs of a high order.

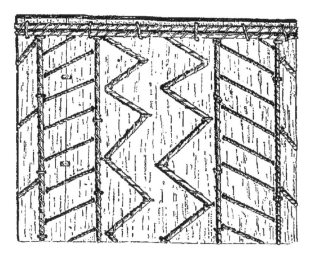

FIG. 357. Portion of a tapa stamp, showing its subtextile character. A palm leaf is cut to the desired shape and the patterns are sewed in or stitched on.

FIG. 358. Design in stucco, exhibiting textile characters.

The ancient "hall of the arabesques" at Chimu, Peru, is decorated in elaborate designs that could only have arisen in the textile art (Fig. 358), and other equally striking examples are to be found in other American countries. The classic surface decorations known and used in Oriental countries from time immemorial prevailed in indigenous American architecture at a stage of culture lower than any known stage of classic art.

It may appear that I have advocated too strongly the claims of the textile art to the parentage of geometric ornament and that the conclusions reached are not entirely satisfactory, but I have endeavored so to present the varied phenomena of the art that the student may readily reach deductions of his own. A correspondingly careful study of other branches of art will probably enable us finally to form a just estimate of the relative importance of the forces and tendencies concerned in the evolution of decoration.

www.ingramcontent.com/pod-product-compliance
Ingram Content Group UK Ltd.
Pitfield, Milton Keynes, MK11 3LW, UK
UKHW042151281224
453045UK00004B/322